User's Guide For AWOL LTV-3500 Pro

Revealing the Strategies, Tips and Tricks for Mastering the Projector

By

Kevin Editions

Table Of Contents

Introduction

Get ready to rumble! This is your User's Guide for the AWOL LTV-3500 Pro projector. In this comprehensive user manual, we will talk about strategies, tips and tricks that will help you take full control of this advanced projector and make it possible to enjoy an amazing home cinema experience. We have tailored this book for you whether you are a pro who knows how to get everything that his/her projects cost or a beginner who is interested in realizing the true potential of their investment so as to make them a go-to resource on how to maximize the capabilities of AWOL LTV-3500 Pro.

Unleashing the Power of Projection

The advent of digital technology has seen home entertainment change significantly with movies being projected at home using projectors. The AWOL LTV-3500 Pro is an innovative technology that promises nothing less than turning around your viewing experiences.

What to Expect

To better understand all functions, features and settings within AWOL LTV-3500 Pro projectors, this guide offers a step by step process which includes options in cut-off points called "the end". To start with, we will give you some basic information on how to install and connect it so that you begin from somewhere. Then we will examine different properties of the projector – such as image quality adjustments, audio configurations and connectivity options.

Unveiling the Secrets to Achieving the Best Performance

One of the major objectives of this book is to offer you ways of improving the performance of AWOL LTV-3500 Pro projector. We will help you realize your goal whether it is for a clear picture, sound that blows your mind or connection with other peripheral devices.

Unwrapping Hints and Techniques

Besides strategies, we also present a gold mine of hints and techniques that improve your overall user experience. Referencing valuable shortcuts and methods on customizing settings for different content types, using the menu system efficiently, will make the projector's interaction easier.

Becoming an Expert on Projector Use

After reading this guide, you will be very conversant with AWOL LTV-3500 Pro projector plus all its possibilities. If you are watching movies during weekends; playing games or conducting business presentations then this knowledge gives you abilities to use it to its ultimate advantage.

Who is this book for?

This manual is meant to help anyone who has or intends to have the AWOL LTV-3500 Pro projector. It is intended for home theater fans, game enthusiasts, and business people among others in a very wide range of users looking to get the most out of their projectors.

Let's Begin 💪!

Without wasting more time let us now start our expedition on understanding and mastering the AWOL LTV-3500 Pro Projector. Be prepared to discover the techniques, advice and hints that will change your experience in watching movies and elevate your entertainment!

Chapter 1: Getting Started

Unboxing and Initial setup

Setting up and unboxing the AWOL LTV-3500 Pro projector is a simple and fun process that enables users to start enjoying high-quality visual experiences fast. In this part, we shall go through the steps of unboxing the projectors and setting them up for optimal performance.

The first step in starting with the AWOL LTV-3500 Pro is through unboxing it. As you gently unwrap it, you will notice it kept safely in a carton alongside other necessary items like remote control, power cable, user manual or extra items such as streaming stick or cables if any.

At this point you can commence on your initial setup after laying out all components. Commence by looking for an ideal place to install your projector. The LTV-3500 Pro offers flexibility in terms of positioning as you may choose to locate it on a TV stand or have it mounted on the ceiling depending on your preference or room layout. Make sure that this area has enough ventilation and allows for clear projection by the machine.

After that, you have to link the power line with the projector and then connect it to an electric socket. To switch on the device, use either a power button located on its body or on your remote control. Once you do this, your projector's start-up screen will appear.

You will be guided through a setup menu that provides various options for personalizing your projector as per your requirements. It involves choosing the right language, altering display settings like aspect ratio and resolution as well as configuring network settings throughout internet connectivity.

For those who are using external devices such as streaming sticks, gaming consoles or Blu-ray players with their projectors, they can connect to the relevant ports (HDMI, USB etc.) of their projectors using appropriate cables. HDMI ports are multiple in LTV-3500 Pro besides many more USB ports and Ethernet connection and optical audio input which give a wide range of connections for different appliances.

Now that the physical connections are complete one may need to adjust some projector settings before starting watching movies. When you press a certain key on your remote control device you will see more advanced display options or even color calibration among other things while just being within an on-screen menu.

Short-throw is one of the features that defines LTV-3500 Pro; thus, it projects a huge screen even in small spaces. Bear in mind factors like ambient light and viewing angles as you adjust the distance between your projector and wall or screen to get your desired screen size.

Now, familiarize yourself with the remote control and projector interface whilst doing the initial setup and configuration. Furthermore, menu navigation onscreen control volume input selection can also be handled by this device acting like a remote.

After unboxing and setting up the AWOL LTV-3500 Pro projector, you are ready to begin exploring vibrant visuals, immersive audio, and engaging entertainment experiences. As such, whether you are watching movies, gaming or streaming favorite contents; LTV-3500 Pro will always ensure outstanding performance and flexibility; thereby rendering it an invaluable asset for any home entertainment system.

Connecting the Projector to Power and Devices

To ensure that the AWOL LTV 3500 Pro projector is well powered and can receive signals from other devices, it is necessary to connect this system to a power source and other gadgets. The steps involved in connecting the projector to power and other devices are discussed here.

Firstly, get hold of the original charger that comes with your AWOL LTV-3500 Pro projector. Normally, the power cable will have a standard plug that can be connected to any electricity socket. Make sure you place your projector near a wall outlet for easy access to its effective power supply.

After having found both the charger cable and an available electrical socket, insert one end of the charger cord into the power input port on the back or side of your projector which should be located alongside HDMI and USB ports.

Once this is done securely attach it to another electric pole nearby and ensure it's switched on so that there would be no problem with delivering energy required by this device.

The projector is connected to power and now you can begin connecting it to other devices such as streaming sticks, gaming consoles, Blu-ray players, laptops, or desktop computers. The AWOL LTV-3500 Pro has many ways for you to connect different devices.

You must use the right cables when attaching external devices like streaming sticks or gaming consoles to your projector; for example HDMI cables, USB cables and optical audio cable. This projector comes with several HDMI ports, USB ports, Ethernet connection and optical audio input that makes its connectivity options versatile.

To connect using HDMI first identify the HDMI port on the projector then plug one end of the HDMI cable into it. After which plug in the other end of the cable into the device's HDMI port. Repeat this process for every device you need to connect to your projector.

Devices that require sound output such as gaming consoles or blu-ray players can be connected to external speakers or a sound system with audio cables. It has an optical audio input that supports high-quality audio output making it perfect for watching movies or playing games in full immersion mode.

Power on all the devices once they are connected to the projector and you select the right input source using the projector. Using either remote control or on-screen menu, navigate to your input selection option followed by selecting your related input sources for all devices that have been connected (e.g., HDMI 1, HDMI 2, USB etc.).

Once properly connected to power and devices, this enables you to enjoy watching your favorite content on a wider screen with more image quality as well as sound effects than before. The easy connections of AWOL LTV-3500 Pro facilitate smooth installation without any hindrances thus enabling different forms of amusement for customers.

Turning on and Navigating the Menu

Turning on the AWOL LTV-3500 Pro projector and navigating its menu are essential steps to begin using its features effectively. In this section, we will explore the process of turning on the projector and navigating through its menu to access various settings and functions.

To start, ensure that the projector is connected to power and that all necessary devices, such as streaming sticks, gaming consoles, or Blu-ray players, are also connected and powered on. Once everything is set up, you can proceed to turn on the projector.

The AWOL LTV-3500 Pro projector can be turned on using either the power button located on the device itself or the power button on the remote control. Press the power button once to turn on the projector. You will see the projector's startup screen, indicating that it is powering up and initializing its systems.

As the projector boots up, you will be greeted with the projector's main menu or home screen. The main menu provides access to various settings, options, and features of the projector, allowing you to customize your viewing experience according to your preferences.

Navigate through the menu using the remote control's arrow keys or directional pad. The remote control typically has dedicated buttons for navigation, menu access, and selection, making it easy to move around the menu and select options.

The main menu of the AWOL LTV-3500 Pro projector is organized into different categories or sections, each containing specific settings and functions. Common menu categories include:

1. Picture Settings: Adjust display settings such as brightness, contrast, color temperature, sharpness, aspect ratio, and picture mode (e.g., standard, cinema, game mode).

2. Audio Settings: Customize audio settings such as volume, equalizer settings, surround sound modes, audio output options, and speaker configuration.

3. Input Selection: Choose the input source for the projector, such as HDMI inputs, USB inputs, Ethernet connection, or wireless connectivity options (Wi-Fi, Bluetooth).

4. Network Settings: Configure network settings for internet connectivity, including Wi-Fi setup, Ethernet connection, IP address settings, and network status.

5. System Settings: Access system settings such as language preferences, time and date settings, firmware updates, factory reset options, and system information.

6. Advanced Settings: Explore advanced settings and features of the projector, including 3D settings (if supported), keystone correction, color management, projector orientation, and more.

Use the arrow keys on the remote control to navigate through the menu categories and submenus. Press the "OK" or "Enter" button to select an option or enter a submenu. You can also use the "Back" or "Exit" button to return to the previous menu or exit a submenu.

As you navigate through the menu, familiarize yourself with the available settings and options. Adjust display settings to optimize picture quality, configure audio settings for immersive sound, select input sources for connected devices, and explore advanced settings for additional customization.

Once you have configured the desired settings and options, you can start enjoying your favorite content on the big screen with the AWOL LTV-3500 Pro projector. The intuitive menu navigation and user-friendly interface make it easy to access and adjust settings for an enhanced viewing experience.

Chapter 2: Understanding the Features

Exploring the Projector's Specifications

Exploring the specifications of the AWOL LTV-3500 Pro projector provides valuable insights into its capabilities, performance, and suitability for various use cases. In this section, we will delve into the key specifications of the projector, including display technology, resolution, brightness, connectivity options, and more.

Display Technology

The AWOL LTV-3500 Pro projector utilizes advanced display technology to deliver stunning visual experiences. It features DLP (Digital Light Processing) technology, known for its high image quality, color accuracy, and reliability. DLP technology uses microscopic mirrors to create images, resulting in sharp details, vibrant colors, and smooth motion rendering.

Resolution

One of the standout features of the LTV-3500 Pro projector is its impressive resolution capabilities. It supports native 4K Ultra HD resolution, offering four times the detail and clarity of Full HD (1080p) resolution. The native 4K resolution ensures crisp and lifelike image reproduction, making it ideal for watching movies, gaming, and viewing high-resolution content.

Brightness

The projector's brightness level is a crucial factor in determining its performance in various lighting conditions. The AWOL LTV-3500 Pro boasts a high brightness rating of 3,500 ANSI lumens. This brightness level ensures vibrant and clear images even in well-lit environments or rooms with ambient light. Whether you're watching movies during the day or gaming at night, the projector maintains excellent visibility and image quality.

Contrast Ratio

Another important specification to consider is the projector's contrast ratio, which affects the depth and richness of colors in images. The LTV-3500 Pro offers a high contrast ratio of X:1, ensuring deep blacks, bright whites, and a wide range of grayscale tones. This high contrast ratio enhances the overall image quality, especially in scenes with high dynamic range (HDR) content.

Throw Ratio and Screen Size

The throw ratio of a projector determines the distance required to achieve a specific screen size. The LTV-3500 Pro features a short-throw design, allowing it to project large screen sizes from a relatively short distance. With a throw ratio of X:X, the projector can produce screen sizes ranging from XX inches to XX inches, making it suitable for small to medium-sized rooms.

Refresh Rate and Response Time

For gaming enthusiasts, the refresh rate and response time of the projector are crucial specifications. The LTV-3500 Pro supports a refresh rate of XX Hz, ensuring smooth and fluid motion playback, especially in fast-paced games and action scenes. The projector's response time of XX milliseconds minimizes input lag, resulting in responsive gaming experiences without noticeable delays.

Connectivity Options

The LTV-3500 Pro offers a wide range of connectivity options to accommodate various devices and sources. It includes multiple HDMI ports, USB ports, an Ethernet connection, optical audio input, and wireless connectivity options such as Wi-Fi and Bluetooth. These connectivity options enable seamless integration with gaming consoles, streaming devices, Blu-ray players, laptops, and more.

Additional Features

In addition to the core specifications mentioned above, the AWOL LTV-3500 Pro projector may include additional features and functionalities. These may include support for HDR (High Dynamic Range) content, 3D capability (if supported), keystone correction, lens shift, built-in speakers, smart TV integration, and compatibility with voice assistants.

Overall, exploring the specifications of the AWOL LTV-3500 Pro projector provides users with a comprehensive understanding of its technical capabilities and performance attributes. Whether you're a movie enthusiast, gamer, or multimedia enthusiast, the projector's specifications ensure an immersive and enjoyable viewing experience.

Overview of the Remote Control

The remote control is an essential component of the AWOL LTV-3500 Pro projector, providing users with convenient access to various functions, settings, and controls. In this section, we will provide an overview of the remote control, highlighting its design, buttons, functionalities, and how to use it effectively.

Design

The remote control for the LTV-3500 Pro projector features a sleek and ergonomic design, making it comfortable to hold and operate for extended periods. It is lightweight yet durable, with a well-built construction that ensures reliability and longevity. The compact size of the remote control makes it easy to handle and store when not in use.

Buttons and Layout

The remote control is equipped with a range of buttons and controls that allow users to navigate through menus, adjust settings, change input sources, control playback, and more. The layout of the buttons is intuitive and user-friendly, designed to facilitate effortless operation of the projector.

Here are the key buttons and controls found on the remote control:

1. Power Button: Turns the projector on or off.
2. Navigation Arrows: Allow navigation through menus and options.
3. OK/Enter Button: Confirms selections or enters submenu options.
4. Menu Button: Opens the main menu for accessing settings and options.
5. Source/Input Button: Changes input sources for the projector (HDMI, USB, etc.).
6. Volume Controls: Adjusts the volume level of the projector's built-in speakers or external audio output.
7. Mute Button: Mutes or unmutes audio output.

8. Playback Controls (if applicable): Play, Pause, Stop, Rewind, Fast Forward buttons for media playback.

9. Aspect Ratio Button: Adjusts the aspect ratio of the projected image (16:9, 4:3, etc.).

10. Picture Mode Button: Switches between different picture modes (Standard, Cinema, Game, etc.).

11. Audio Mode Button: Switches between different audio modes (Stereo, Surround, etc.).

12. Back/Exit Button: Returns to the previous menu or exits a submenu.

13. Info Button: Displays information about the current content or settings.

14. Settings Button: Accesses advanced settings and options for the projector.

15. Numeric Keypad: Allows direct input of numeric values or selections.

Functionality

The remote control provides comprehensive functionality for controlling all aspects of the projector's operation. Users can power the projector on or off, navigate through menus, adjust picture and audio settings, switch input sources, control media playback, and access advanced settings with ease.

To use the remote control effectively, aim it towards the front or infrared sensor of the projector, ensuring a clear line of sight for optimal signal transmission. Press the desired button or control to activate the corresponding function or setting on the projector.

The remote control's navigation arrows allow users to move up, down, left, or right within menus and options. The OK/Enter button confirms selections or enters submenu options, while the Back/Exit button returns to the previous menu or exits a submenu.

Users can adjust volume levels using the volume controls, mute or unmute audio using the mute button, and switch between different input sources using the source/input button. The remote control also includes dedicated buttons for adjusting aspect ratio, picture mode, and audio mode, providing quick access to commonly used settings.

The remote control of the AWOL LTV-3500 Pro projector is an intuitive and versatile tool that enhances the user experience by offering convenient control and customization options. Its ergonomic design, comprehensive layout, and functional buttons make it an essential accessory for operating the projector efficiently.

Key features and Functions Explained

The AWOL LTV-3500 Pro projector is packed with key features and functions that enhance its performance, versatility, and user experience. In this section, we will explore and explain these key features and functions in detail, providing insights into how they contribute to the projector's capabilities and usability.

1. Native 4K Ultra HD Resolution

One of the standout features of the LTV-3500 Pro projector is its native 4K Ultra HD resolution. This high-resolution capability ensures crisp, detailed, and lifelike image reproduction with four times the clarity of Full HD (1080p) resolution. Whether you're watching movies, gaming, or viewing high-resolution content, the native 4K resolution delivers stunning visuals and immersive viewing experiences.

2. DLP Display Technology

The projector utilizes DLP (Digital Light Processing) technology, known for its high image quality, color accuracy, and reliability. DLP technology uses microscopic mirrors to create images, resulting in sharp details, vibrant colors, and smooth motion rendering. This advanced display technology enhances the overall visual performance of the projector, making it suitable for a wide range of multimedia applications.

3. High Brightness and Contrast Ratio

The LTV-3500 Pro projector boasts a high brightness rating of 3,500 ANSI lumens, ensuring vibrant and clear images even in well-lit environments or rooms with ambient light. Additionally, it features a high contrast ratio, producing deep blacks, bright whites, and a wide range of grayscale tones for enhanced image depth and richness. These brightness and contrast capabilities contribute to an excellent viewing experience across various lighting conditions.

4. Short-Throw Design

The projector's short-throw design allows it to project large screen sizes from a relatively short distance. This makes it suitable for small to medium-sized rooms where space constraints may be a consideration. The short-throw design minimizes the distance required between the projector and the screen, providing flexibility in placement and setup options.

5. Versatile Connectivity Options

The LTV-3500 Pro offers a wide range of connectivity options to accommodate various devices and sources. It includes multiple HDMI ports, USB ports, an Ethernet connection, optical audio input, and wireless connectivity options such as Wi-Fi and Bluetooth. These connectivity options enable seamless integration with gaming consoles, streaming devices, Blu-ray players, laptops, and more, enhancing the projector's versatility and compatibility.

6. Advanced Picture and Audio Settings

The projector's menu system includes advanced picture and audio settings that allow users to customize their viewing and listening experiences. Users can adjust display settings such as brightness, contrast, color temperature, sharpness, aspect ratio, and picture mode to optimize picture quality. Similarly, audio settings such as volume, equalizer settings, surround sound modes, and speaker configuration can be adjusted to suit individual preferences.

7. Built-In Speakers and Audio Output

The LTV-3500 Pro projector features built-in speakers that deliver clear and immersive audio output. Users can enjoy audio directly from the projector's speakers or connect external audio devices such as soundbars, speakers, or home theater systems for enhanced audio performance. The projector's audio output options ensure a complete multimedia experience with rich and dynamic sound quality.

8. Smart Home Integration and Control

The projector supports smart home integration and control, allowing users to connect and control compatible smart home devices and systems. This includes integration with voice assistants such as Amazon Alexa or Google

Assistant, enabling voice commands for projector operation, content playback, and settings adjustments. Smart home integration adds convenience and accessibility to the projector's functionalities, enhancing the overall user experience.

9. Keystone Correction and Lens Shift

The LTV-3500 Pro projector includes keystone correction and lens shift features that help adjust the projected image for optimal viewing. Keystone correction corrects image distortion caused by angled projection, ensuring a straight and rectangular image on the screen. Lens shift allows users to adjust the position of the projected image vertically or horizontally without physically moving the projector, providing flexibility in screen placement and alignment.

10. Gaming and Multimedia Capabilities

For gaming enthusiasts, the projector offers gaming-specific features such as low input lag, high refresh rates, and smooth motion rendering. The low input lag minimizes delays between user input and on-screen response, enhancing gaming responsiveness. Additionally, the high refresh rates ensure smooth and fluid motion playback, ideal for fast-paced gaming and multimedia content.

11. User-Friendly Interface and Remote Control

The projector's user interface is designed to be intuitive and user-friendly, making it easy to navigate menus, access settings, and control functions. The included remote control provides convenient access to various features and controls, allowing users to operate the projector effortlessly from a distance. The combination of a user-friendly interface and remote control enhances the overall usability and accessibility of the projector.

The AWOL LTV-3500 Pro projector offers a comprehensive array of key features and functions that cater to diverse user needs and preferences. From its native 4K resolution and advanced display technology to its versatile connectivity options, audio capabilities, smart home integration, and gaming/multimedia capabilities, the projector delivers an exceptional viewing and entertainment experience.

Chapter 3: Optimizing Picture Quality

Adjusting Brightness, Contrast, and Color Settings

Adjusting brightness, contrast, and color settings on the AWOL LTV-3500 Pro projector is essential to optimize the visual quality and enhance the viewing experience. In this section, we will delve into the process of adjusting these settings, exploring their impact on image quality and providing guidelines for achieving the desired display characteristics.

1. Brightness Adjustment

Brightness refers to the overall intensity of light emitted by the projector, affecting the visibility and clarity of the projected image. Adjusting the brightness setting allows users to control the level of luminance or brightness in the image. Here's how to adjust brightness on the LTV-3500 Pro projector:

- Navigate to the projector's menu using the remote control or on-screen display.
- Select the "Picture" or "Display" settings menu, depending on the menu structure.
- Look for the "Brightness" or "Luminance" option within the picture settings.
- Use the navigation arrows on the remote control to increase or decrease the brightness level.

- Preview the changes on the screen and adjust until the desired brightness is achieved.

Increasing brightness can make the image appear brighter and more vibrant, ideal for well-lit environments or scenes with bright content. Decreasing brightness can reduce glare and eye strain, suitable for dimly lit rooms or nighttime viewing.

2. Contrast Adjustment

Contrast refers to the difference in brightness between the brightest and darkest parts of the image, influencing the depth and richness of colors and details. Adjusting the contrast setting allows users to enhance the image's overall contrast ratio for better visual impact. Here's how to adjust contrast on the LTV-3500 Pro projector:

- Access the projector's menu and navigate to the "Picture" or "Display" settings menu.
- Locate the "Contrast" or "Contrast Ratio" option within the picture settings.
- Use the navigation arrows on the remote control to increase or decrease the contrast level.
- Fine-tune the contrast setting to achieve a balanced and natural-looking image with adequate detail in both dark and bright areas.

Increasing contrast can make colors appear more vivid and details more pronounced, enhancing image clarity and depth. However, excessive contrast adjustments may lead to overblown highlights or crushed shadows, affecting overall image quality.

3. Color Settings Adjustment

Color settings encompass a range of parameters such as color temperature, color saturation, hue, and color space, allowing users to customize the projector's color reproduction to their preferences. Here's how to adjust color settings on the LTV-3500 Pro projector:

- Enter the projector's menu and navigate to the "Color" or "Color Settings" menu.
- Explore options such as "Color Temperature," "Color Saturation," "Hue," and "Color Space."
- Adjust color temperature to control the overall warmth or coolness of the colors.
- Modify color saturation to enhance or reduce the intensity of colors.
- Fine-tune hue settings for precise color balance and accuracy.
- Select the appropriate color space (e.g., Standard, Cinema, Game) based on content type and personal preference.

Adjusting color settings allows users to achieve accurate color reproduction, vibrant visuals, and color consistency across different media sources. Calibrating color settings according to the content type (e.g., movies, games, presentations) can enhance the overall viewing experience.

4. Advanced Picture Mode Settings

The LTV-3500 Pro projector may offer advanced picture mode settings such as "Standard," "Cinema," "Game," "Dynamic," and "User" modes. Each mode may have predefined settings for brightness, contrast, color temperature, and other parameters optimized for specific viewing scenarios. Users can choose the appropriate picture mode based on their content and viewing environment preferences.

- Navigate to the projector's menu and select the "Picture Mode" or "Viewing Mode" option.
- Choose from available picture modes such as Standard, Cinema, Game, Dynamic, or User mode.
- Customize settings within the selected picture mode, such as brightness, contrast, color, and sharpness.

- Experiment with different picture modes to find the one that best suits your viewing preferences and content type.

5. Calibration and Fine-Tuning

For users seeking precise calibration and fine-tuning of brightness, contrast, and color settings, the LTV-3500 Pro projector may offer advanced calibration tools or access to professional calibration services. Calibration tools include grayscale adjustments, gamma settings, color management systems (CMS), and white balance controls for achieving accurate and calibrated colors.

- Access advanced calibration settings within the projector's menu or settings submenu.
- Use calibration tools such as grayscale patterns, color test patterns, and calibration software for precise adjustments.

- Follow calibration guides or consult professional calibration services for expert-level adjustments and optimization.

Fine-tuning brightness, contrast, and color settings on the AWOL LTV-3500 Pro projector allows users to customize their viewing experience, achieve optimal image quality, and enjoy immersive visuals across different content types and viewing environments. Experimenting with various settings, picture modes, and calibration tools can help users find the perfect balance of brightness, contrast, and color reproduction for an enhanced cinematic experience or gaming immersion.

Fine-tuning the Picture for Different Viewing Environments

Fine-tuning the picture settings on the AWOL LTV-3500 Pro projector for different viewing environments is crucial to ensure optimal image quality, clarity, and visual comfort. In this section, we will discuss the process of fine-tuning the picture settings to suit various viewing environments, including dark rooms, well-lit spaces, and gaming setups.

1. Dark Room Settings

For viewing in dark or low-light environments such as dedicated home theaters or nighttime settings, adjusting the picture settings for optimal performance is essential. Here are the recommended settings for dark room viewing on the LTV-3500 Pro projector:

- Brightness: Set the brightness level to a moderate level that provides adequate visibility without causing eye strain. Avoid setting brightness too high, as it can lead to glare or discomfort in dark environments.
- Contrast: Increase the contrast level to enhance image depth and richness,

ensuring clear distinction between dark and bright areas of the image.

- Color Temperature: Choose a color temperature setting that suits your preference for warm or cool colors. A slightly warmer color temperature may enhance viewing comfort in dark rooms.
- Color Saturation: Adjust color saturation to a level that brings out vibrant colors without oversaturating or distorting the image.
- Gamma Correction: Fine-tune gamma settings to optimize grayscale performance and ensure smooth tonal transitions, especially in dark scenes.
- Picture Mode: Select a picture mode optimized for dark room viewing, such as Cinema or Movie mode, which typically offers calibrated settings for enhanced contrast and color accuracy.

By fine-tuning these picture settings, users can enjoy immersive and cinematic experiences in dark room environments, with enhanced image quality, deep blacks, and accurate colors.

2. Well-Lit Room Settings

In brightly lit or ambient light environments such as living rooms, conference rooms, or classrooms, adjusting the picture settings is essential to maintain image visibility, clarity, and contrast. Here are the recommended settings for well-lit room viewing on the LTV-3500 Pro projector:

- Brightness: Increase the brightness level to ensure adequate visibility of the image in well-lit environments. Adjust brightness according to ambient light conditions to avoid washed-out or dim visuals.
- Contrast: Maintain a balanced contrast level that preserves detail and clarity in both dark and bright areas of the image, without sacrificing overall brightness.

- Color Temperature: Choose a color temperature setting that complements the ambient lighting conditions. A slightly cooler color temperature may help counterbalance warm ambient light.
- Color Saturation: Adjust color saturation to maintain vibrant colors and prevent colors from appearing washed out or dull in bright environments.
- Ambient Light Sensor (if available): Some projectors may feature ambient light sensors that automatically adjust brightness and color settings based on ambient light conditions. Enable this feature for automatic optimization in varying lighting environments.

By optimizing these picture settings, users can enjoy clear, vibrant, and well-defined visuals in well-lit rooms, ensuring an engaging viewing experience for presentations, multimedia content, and daytime viewing.

3. Gaming Setup Settings

For gaming enthusiasts, fine-tuning the picture settings on the LTV-3500 Pro projector for gaming setups is essential to achieve optimal performance, responsiveness, and visual quality. Here are the recommended settings for gaming setups on the projector:

- Input Lag: Enable gaming mode or low input lag settings to minimize input delay and ensure responsive gameplay, especially in fast-paced games.
- Refresh Rate: Set the refresh rate to match the gaming console or PC output for smooth and fluid motion rendering during gameplay.
- Color Accuracy: Adjust color settings for accurate color reproduction, vibrant visuals, and enhanced gaming immersion. Avoid oversaturation or color distortion that may affect gameplay visibility.
- Motion Smoothing: Disable motion smoothing or interpolation features that

may introduce input lag or motion artifacts during gaming.

- Game Mode: Activate game-specific picture modes or presets that optimize settings for gaming, such as reduced input lag, enhanced contrast, and sharpness adjustments.

By fine-tuning these picture settings specifically for gaming setups, users can enjoy responsive, immersive, and visually stunning gaming experiences on the LTV-3500 Pro projector, with optimized settings for different gaming genres and preferences.

4. Customized Presets and Profiles

The LTV-3500 Pro projector may offer customizable presets or user profiles that allow users to save and recall preferred picture settings for different viewing environments or content types. Users can create custom presets for dark room viewing, well-lit environments, gaming setups, movie nights, presentations, and more, ensuring quick and easy access to optimized settings based on specific needs.

- Create Custom Presets: Access the projector's menu or settings to create custom presets or profiles.
- Save Preferred Settings: Adjust picture settings according to each viewing environment or content type, and save them as custom presets for future use.
- Recall Presets: Easily switch between preset profiles using the remote control or menu options, allowing instant optimization for different scenarios without manual adjustments.

By utilizing customized presets and profiles, users can streamline the process of adjusting picture settings for different viewing environments, ensuring consistent performance, and tailored visual experiences across various usage scenarios.

Fine-tuning the picture settings on the AWOL LTV-3500 Pro projector for different viewing environments is essential to achieve optimal image quality, clarity, and visual comfort. By adjusting settings such as brightness, contrast, color temperature, and gamma correction, users can customize their viewing experiences for dark rooms, well-lit spaces, gaming setups, and more, ensuring immersive and enjoyable viewing experiences across a range of scenarios.

Using Presets for Different Content Types (movies, games, etc.)

Using presets for different content types such as movies, games, presentations, and more on the AWOL LTV-3500 Pro projector enhances the viewing experience by optimizing picture settings specific to each content category. Presets offer convenience, efficiency, and tailored performance for various media types, ensuring accurate color reproduction, enhanced contrast, and optimal visual quality. In this section, we will explore the benefits of using presets and how to leverage them effectively for different content types.

1. Movie Mode Preset

The Movie mode preset on the LTV-3500 Pro projector is designed to deliver cinematic viewing experiences with optimized settings for movies, TV shows, and video content. Here's how to use the Movie mode preset effectively:

- Access the projector's menu and navigate to the picture settings or viewing mode options.
- Select the Movie mode preset from the available presets or picture modes list.
- The Movie mode preset typically adjusts settings such as color temperature, contrast, sharpness, and gamma to enhance cinematic visuals.
- Enjoy enhanced color accuracy, deep blacks, and detailed images suitable for

movie watching in dark or dimly lit environments.

The Movie mode preset is ideal for immersive movie nights, streaming services, and home theater setups, providing a cinematic experience with rich colors, accurate skin tones, and enhanced contrast for a captivating viewing experience.

2. Game Mode Preset

The Game mode preset on the LTV-3500 Pro projector is optimized for gaming experiences, offering reduced input lag, enhanced motion clarity, and responsive gameplay visuals. Here's how to use the Game mode preset effectively:

- Navigate to the projector's menu and select the picture settings or gaming mode options.
- Choose the Game mode preset from the available presets or gaming modes list.

- The Game mode preset typically prioritizes settings such as refresh rate, input lag reduction, color accuracy, and motion smoothing for optimal gaming performance.
- Experience smooth, fluid gameplay with minimal input delay, vibrant colors, and sharp visuals suitable for gaming setups and console gaming.

The Game mode preset enhances gaming immersion, responsiveness, and visual quality, making it ideal for gamers seeking an optimized gaming experience without compromising on image quality or performance.

3. Presentation Mode Preset

The Presentation mode preset on the LTV-3500 Pro projector is tailored for professional presentations, business meetings, educational content, and slideshows. Here's how to use the Presentation mode preset effectively:

- Access the projector's menu and navigate to the picture settings or presentation mode options.
- Select the Presentation mode preset from the available presets or presentation modes list.
- The Presentation mode preset typically optimizes settings such as brightness, color saturation, sharpness, and gamma for clear text, vibrant graphics, and impactful presentations.
- Deliver professional presentations with enhanced visibility, sharp details, and accurate color reproduction suitable for various business and educational environments.

The Presentation mode preset ensures clear, legible text, vivid graphics, and optimal contrast for engaging and effective presentations, making it a valuable tool for professionals and educators.

4. Custom User Presets

The LTV-3500 Pro projector may offer customizable user presets or profiles that allow users to create and save their preferred settings for different content types or viewing scenarios. Here's how to create and use custom user presets effectively:

- Access the projector's menu or settings and navigate to the custom presets or user profiles section.
- Create a new user preset and adjust picture settings such as brightness, contrast, color temperature, and sharpness according to your preferences.
- Save the customized settings as a new user preset for quick and easy access in the future.
- Switch between custom user presets based on the content type (movies, games, presentations) or viewing environment (dark room, well-lit room) for personalized and optimized performance.

Custom user presets offer flexibility, customization, and personalized optimization for specific content types, viewing preferences, and usage scenarios, allowing users to tailor their viewing experiences to their liking.

Using presets for different content types on the AWOL LTV-3500 Pro projector enhances convenience, efficiency, and performance by optimizing picture settings for movies, games, presentations, and more. Leveraging presets such as Movie mode, Game mode, Presentation mode, and custom user presets ensures accurate color reproduction, enhanced contrast, reduced input lag, and optimal visual quality across various media types and viewing environments, delivering immersive and engaging viewing experiences tailored to individual preferences.

Chapter 4: Audio Setup

Connecting External Speakers or Sound Systems

Connecting external speakers or sound systems to the AWOL LTV-3500 Pro projector enhances audio performance, immersion, and overall viewing experience, especially for movies, gaming, and multimedia content. In this section, we will explore the process of connecting external speakers or sound systems to the projector, including options for wired and wireless setups, audio configuration settings, and optimizing sound quality.

1. Wired Connection

Connecting external speakers or sound systems to the LTV-3500 Pro projector using a wired connection offers reliable audio transmission and flexibility in speaker placement. Follow these steps to connect external speakers via a wired connection:

- Identify the audio output ports on the projector, which may include HDMI ARC (Audio Return Channel), optical audio output, or analog audio output (3.5mm audio jack).
- Choose the appropriate audio output port based on your speaker or sound system's input options. For example, if your speakers support HDMI ARC, connect an HDMI cable from the projector's HDMI ARC port to the HDMI input on the speakers.
- Alternatively, if your speakers have optical audio input, use an optical audio cable to connect the projector's optical audio output to the optical input on the speakers.
- For analog audio output, use a 3.5mm audio cable to connect the projector's audio output jack to the audio input on the speakers or sound system.

- Once the physical connections are made, configure the projector's audio settings to output audio through the connected external speakers. Access the projector's audio settings menu and select the appropriate audio output source (HDMI ARC, optical, or analog).

By establishing a wired connection between the projector and external speakers, users can enjoy enhanced audio quality, immersive surround sound, and precise audio synchronization for an immersive viewing experience.

2. Wireless Connection

For a wireless setup, the LTV-3500 Pro projector may support Bluetooth or Wi-Fi connectivity options for pairing with compatible wireless speakers or sound systems. Here's how to connect external speakers wirelessly to the projector:

- Ensure that both the projector and wireless speakers are powered on and in pairing mode.
- Access the projector's Bluetooth or Wi-Fi settings menu and enable wireless audio output or pairing mode.
- Search for available Bluetooth or Wi-Fi devices on the projector and select the desired wireless speakers or sound system for pairing.
- Follow the on-screen instructions to complete the pairing process between the projector and wireless speakers.
- Once paired, configure the projector's audio settings to route audio output to the connected wireless speakers or sound system.

Wireless connectivity offers convenience, flexibility, and clutter-free audio setups, allowing users to enjoy high-quality audio without physical cables or limitations in speaker placement.

3. Audio Configuration Settings

After connecting external speakers or sound systems to the LTV-3500 Pro projector, users can further optimize audio performance and settings for a customized listening experience. Here are key audio configuration settings to consider:

- Audio Output Selection: Choose the audio output source (external speakers, HDMI ARC, optical, analog) in the projector's audio settings menu to route audio accordingly.
- Sound Modes: Select predefined sound modes or equalizer settings (such as Music, Movie, Game, Dialogue, etc.) to adjust audio characteristics based on the content type or user preferences.
- Volume Control: Adjust the volume levels for the connected external speakers or sound system using the projector's remote control or audio settings menu.
- Audio Delay Correction: If experiencing audio-video sync issues, adjust the audio

delay or synchronization settings in the projector's audio menu to align audio and video playback.

By fine-tuning audio configuration settings, users can achieve optimal sound quality, balance, and immersion when using external speakers or sound systems with the LTV-3500 Pro projector.

Connecting external speakers or sound systems to the AWOL LTV-3500 Pro projector enhances audio performance, immersion, and viewing experience for movies, gaming, presentations, and multimedia content. Whether using a wired or wireless setup, users can enjoy high-quality audio, surround sound, and customizable audio settings to create a personalized and immersive audiovisual environment. By following the steps outlined for wired and wireless connections, configuring audio settings, and optimizing sound quality, users can maximize the potential of their projector-sound system setup for an enhanced entertainment and cinematic experience.

Adjusting Audio Settings for Optimal Sound Quality

Adjusting audio settings on the AWOL LTV-3500 Pro projector is crucial for achieving optimal sound quality and enhancing the overall viewing experience. By fine-tuning audio settings, users can customize audio output, balance, clarity, and immersion to suit their preferences and content type. Here are key audio settings to adjust for optimal sound quality:

1. Sound Mode Selection

The projector may offer predefined sound modes or equalizer settings tailored for different content types such as movies, music, games, and presentations. Selecting the appropriate sound mode can enhance audio characteristics and optimize sound quality based on the content being viewed. For example, choosing a Movie mode may emphasize dialogue clarity and surround sound effects for cinematic experiences, while selecting a Music mode may enhance bass and treble frequencies for music playback.

2. Equalizer Settings

Access the projector's equalizer settings to adjust specific audio frequencies (bass, midrange, treble) according to personal preferences or room acoustics. Fine-tuning the equalizer can improve audio balance, clarity, and depth, allowing users to customize sound output for an immersive listening experience.

3. Surround Sound Enhancement

If the projector supports surround sound technologies such as Dolby Audio or DTS:X, enable surround sound enhancement features to create a more expansive and immersive audio environment. Surround sound processing can simulate multi-channel audio effects, spatial cues, and directional sound for a theater-like experience.

4. Volume Control and Dynamic Range

Adjust the volume levels to achieve comfortable listening levels without distortion or clipping. Use dynamic range settings to control the difference between quiet and loud audio passages, ensuring consistent audio levels and preserving audio detail during playback.

5. Audio Delay Correction

If experiencing audio-video sync issues, utilize audio delay correction settings to synchronize audio and video playback accurately. Adjust the audio delay to minimize lip-sync errors and improve overall audiovisual coherence.

By adjusting these audio settings on the LTV-3500 Pro projector, users can optimize sound quality, balance, and immersion for a customized and immersive viewing experience across various content types and listening environments. Regularly fine-tuning audio settings based on preferences and content requirements ensures consistent and high-quality audio performance for enhanced entertainment enjoyment.

Troubleshooting Common Audio Issues

Troubleshooting common audio issues with the AWOL LTV-3500 Pro projector is essential for resolving sound-related problems and ensuring optimal audio performance during viewing sessions. By identifying and addressing common audio issues, users can experience enhanced sound quality, clarity, and immersion. Here are some common audio problems and troubleshooting steps to resolve them effectively:

1. No Audio Output

If there is no audio output from the projector to external speakers or sound systems, follow these troubleshooting steps:

- Check the audio cable connections between the projector and external speakers. Ensure that cables are securely plugged into the correct audio output ports on the projector and input ports on the speakers.
- Verify that the external speakers or sound system are powered on and set to the correct input source corresponding to the projector's audio output.
- Access the projector's audio settings menu and confirm that the audio output source is selected correctly (HDMI ARC, optical, analog) based on the connected external speakers.
- Test audio playback with different content sources (movies, music, games) to ensure that the issue is not content-specific.

2. Low Volume or Distorted Sound

If experiencing low volume levels or distorted sound quality, try these troubleshooting steps:

- Adjust the volume levels on both the projector and external speakers to ensure adequate volume without distortion. Avoid setting volume levels too high, which can cause audio clipping or distortion.
- Check the audio cables for any damage or loose connections. Replace damaged cables and ensure tight connections between the projector and external speakers.
- Verify that the audio source (media player, streaming device) connected to the projector is outputting audio at an appropriate level and without any audio processing issues.
- Access the projector's audio settings menu and adjust equalizer settings to optimize audio balance, clarity, and depth for improved sound quality.

3. Audio Delay or Sync Issues

If experiencing audio delay or synchronization issues (lip-sync errors), follow these troubleshooting steps:

- Check the audio delay or synchronization settings in the projector's audio menu. Adjust the audio delay to align audio and video playback accurately, reducing or eliminating lip-sync errors.
- Ensure that the connected external speakers or sound system do not introduce additional audio delay or processing that may cause synchronization issues.
- Test audio playback with different content types (movies, games, presentations) to identify if the audio delay issue is content-specific or consistent across all sources.
- If using wireless speakers or sound systems, verify that the wireless connection is stable and not causing audio delay or synchronization issues.

4. Surround Sound or Audio Enhancement Not Working

If surround sound or audio enhancement features are not functioning correctly, try these troubleshooting steps:

- Check the projector's audio settings menu for surround sound or audio enhancement options. Ensure that these features are enabled and configured according to preferences.
- Verify that the external speakers or sound system support surround sound formats (Dolby Audio, DTS:X) and are properly configured to receive surround sound signals from the projector.
- Test surround sound or audio enhancement features with compatible content sources (Blu-ray discs, streaming services) to confirm functionality and effectiveness.

- Update the projector's firmware or software to the latest version, as newer updates may include enhancements or bug fixes related to audio processing and surround sound capabilities.

5. Audio Interruptions or Dropouts

If experiencing audio interruptions or dropouts during playback, consider these troubleshooting steps:

- Check for wireless interference or signal strength issues if using wireless speakers or sound systems. Move the projector and wireless devices closer together or eliminate potential sources of interference.
- Ensure that audio cables are in good condition and free from damage or interference. Replace damaged cables and secure connections between the projector and external speakers.
- Test audio playback with different media sources (streaming, Blu-ray, HDMI

inputs) to determine if audio interruptions occur consistently or are specific to certain content sources.

- Adjust audio settings such as audio bitrate, sample rate, and audio processing options in the projector's settings menu to optimize audio stability and reduce dropouts.

By following these troubleshooting steps and addressing common audio issues systematically, users can resolve audio problems effectively and enjoy enhanced sound quality, clarity, and immersion with the AWOL LTV-3500 Pro projector for an optimal viewing experience. Regular maintenance, firmware updates, and proper audio setup contribute to consistent and high-quality audio performance during entertainment and multimedia playback sessions.

Chapter 5: Streaming and Connectivity

Connecting streaming devices like the Fire TV Stick to the AWOL LTV-3500 Pro projector expands entertainment options by enabling access to streaming services, apps, and digital content directly on the projector's large screen. This section provides a comprehensive guide on how to connect and set up streaming devices for seamless playback and content streaming.

1. Choose the Right Streaming Device

Before connecting a streaming device to the projector, select a compatible device that meets your streaming needs and preferences. Popular options include the Amazon Fire TV Stick, Roku Streaming Stick, Google Chromecast, and Apple TV. Consider factors such as content availability, app support, streaming resolution (HD, 4K), and connectivity options.

2. Prepare the Streaming Device

Unbox the streaming device and ensure it includes the necessary components such as the streaming stick, remote control, power adapter, and HDMI extension cable (if required). Familiarize yourself with the device's setup instructions, including Wi-Fi network configuration and account login details for streaming services.

3. Locate HDMI Input on Projector

Identify the HDMI input port on the AWOL LTV-3500 Pro projector where you will connect the streaming device. Most projectors feature multiple HDMI ports labeled HDMI 1, HDMI 2, etc. Choose an available HDMI input port for connecting the streaming device.

4. Connect Streaming Device to Projector

Follow these steps to connect the streaming device to the projector:

- Insert the HDMI connector of the streaming device (e.g., Fire TV Stick) into the selected HDMI input port on the projector.
- If using a streaming stick with a separate power adapter, connect the power adapter to an electrical outlet and plug the USB power cable into the streaming device to provide power.
- Ensure the projector is powered on and select the corresponding HDMI input source (HDMI 1, HDMI 2, etc.) using the projector's remote control or input selection menu.

5. Complete Device Setup

Once the streaming device is connected to the projector, follow the on-screen instructions on the projector's display to complete the device setup process. This may include selecting the language, connecting to a Wi-Fi network, and signing in to your streaming accounts (e.g., Amazon Prime, Netflix, Hulu).

6. Configure Audio Output

Access the projector's audio settings menu to configure audio output settings for the connected streaming device. Choose the appropriate audio output source (HDMI ARC, optical, analog) to route audio from the streaming device to external speakers or sound systems for enhanced sound quality.

7. Install Streaming Apps

After connecting the streaming device, install and launch streaming apps or services directly on the projector. Use the streaming device's remote control to navigate app interfaces, browse content libraries, and start streaming movies, TV shows, music, and more on the big screen.

8. Test Streaming Playback

Verify streaming playback by selecting and playing content from your favorite streaming apps. Ensure smooth playback, high-quality video resolution, and synchronized audio for an immersive viewing experience.

By following these steps, users can successfully connect and set up streaming devices like the Fire TV Stick with the AWOL LTV-3500 Pro projector, unlocking a wide range of streaming content and entertainment options directly on the projector's large screen. Regularly update streaming apps, firmware, and projector settings for optimal streaming performance and compatibility with new streaming services and features.

Using Built-in Streaming Apps

The AWOL LTV-3500 Pro projector comes equipped with built-in streaming apps, offering users convenient access to a variety of digital content, streaming services, and entertainment options directly from the projector's interface. This section provides a detailed guide on how to use and navigate the built-in streaming apps for an immersive and enjoyable streaming experience.

1. Accessing Built-in Streaming Apps

To access the built-in streaming apps on the LTV-3500 Pro projector, follow these steps:

- Power on the projector and navigate to the home screen or main menu using the remote control.
- Locate and select the "Streaming Apps" or "Apps" section on the home screen to view the available built-in streaming apps.
- The projector may include popular streaming apps such as Netflix, Amazon Prime Video, Hulu, YouTube, Disney+, HBO Max, Spotify, and more. Use the remote control to highlight and select the desired app for launching.

2. Logging in or Creating Accounts

If you are using a streaming app that requires a user account or subscription, follow the on-screen prompts to log in to your existing account or create a new account directly from the projector. Use the remote control or on-screen keyboard to enter login credentials, email addresses, and passwords as needed.

3. Navigating App Interfaces

Once inside a streaming app, familiarize yourself with the app's interface and navigation controls. Use the directional buttons on the remote control to navigate menus, browse content categories (Movies, TV Shows, Music, etc.), and select titles for streaming. Some apps may also support voice search or gesture controls for easier navigation.

4. Searching for Content

Use the search feature within streaming apps to quickly find specific movies, TV shows, songs, artists, or genres. Enter keywords or titles using the on-screen keyboard or voice search function (if available) to access content directly.

5. Playing Content

Select a movie, TV show episode, music album, or playlist to start streaming content on the projector's large screen. Use playback controls on the remote control to play, pause, rewind, fast forward, and adjust volume levels during playback. The projector's audio output settings can be adjusted to route audio to external speakers or sound systems for enhanced sound quality.

6. Managing Account Settings

Within each streaming app, access account settings, preferences, and parental controls to customize your streaming experience. Manage playback settings, create watchlists, set up profiles for multiple users, and configure content restrictions for family-friendly viewing.

7. Exiting and Switching Apps

To exit a streaming app and return to the home screen or switch to another app, use the remote control's back button or app switcher function. Navigate between open apps or recently used apps for seamless multitasking and content exploration.

8. Updating Apps and Firmware

Regularly check for app updates and firmware updates for the projector to ensure compatibility, security, and access to new features and content within built-in streaming apps. Follow prompts for app updates or check the projector's settings menu for firmware update options.

By utilizing the built-in streaming apps on the AWOL LTV-3500 Pro projector, users can enjoy a wide range of digital content, streaming services, and entertainment options directly on the big screen without the need for external devices or additional setups. Explore, stream, and discover new content effortlessly for an immersive and cinematic streaming experience from the comfort of your home or entertainment space.

Wireless connectivity options (Wi-Fi, Bluetooth, etc.)

The AWOL LTV-3500 Pro projector offers versatile wireless connectivity options, including Wi-Fi and Bluetooth, to enhance user convenience, expand compatibility with external devices, and streamline multimedia playback and streaming experiences. This section provides an in-depth guide on how to utilize wireless connectivity features on the projector for seamless connectivity and content sharing.

1. Wi-Fi Connectivity

Wi-Fi connectivity enables the projector to connect to wireless networks, access online content, stream media, and facilitate screen mirroring from compatible devices. Follow these steps to utilize Wi-Fi connectivity on the LTV-3500 Pro projector:

- Access the projector's settings menu using the remote control or on-screen interface.
- Navigate to the "Network" or "Wi-Fi" settings section to view available wireless networks.
- Select your Wi-Fi network from the list of available networks and enter the network password (if required) using the on-screen keyboard.
- Once connected to the Wi-Fi network, the projector can access online streaming services, download firmware updates, and enable screen mirroring features for compatible devices.

2. Screen Mirroring (Miracast, AirPlay, Chromecast)

The projector supports screen mirroring technologies such as Miracast (for Android devices), AirPlay (for Apple devices), and Chromecast (for Google devices). Follow these steps to enable screen mirroring on the LTV-3500 Pro projector:

- Ensure that the projector and your compatible device (smartphone, tablet, laptop) are connected to the same Wi-Fi network.
- Access the screen mirroring or casting settings on your device. For Android devices, use the Miracast or Cast feature. For Apple devices, use AirPlay. For Google devices, use Chromecast.
- Select the LTV-3500 Pro projector from the list of available devices for screen mirroring or casting.

- Follow any on-screen prompts to establish a connection between your device and the projector.
- Once connected, your device's screen will be mirrored or cast to the projector's large screen, allowing you to share photos, videos, presentations, and apps wirelessly.

3. Bluetooth Connectivity

Bluetooth connectivity on the projector enables wireless audio streaming and pairing with Bluetooth-enabled devices such as speakers, headphones, and smartphones. Follow these steps to use Bluetooth connectivity on the LTV-3500 Pro projector:

- Access the projector's Bluetooth settings from the settings menu.
- Enable Bluetooth on the projector and set it to discoverable mode.
- On your Bluetooth-enabled device, enable Bluetooth and search for available devices.

- Select the LTV-3500 Pro projector from the list of available Bluetooth devices to pair and connect.
- Once paired, you can stream audio wirelessly from your device to the projector or connect Bluetooth speakers/headphones for enhanced audio playback.

4. Wireless Keyboard and Mouse

For added convenience, the projector supports wireless keyboard and mouse connectivity via USB dongles or Bluetooth. Connect a compatible wireless keyboard and mouse to the projector's USB ports or pair them via Bluetooth to navigate menus, input text, and control applications more efficiently.

5. DLNA and Media Streaming

Utilize DLNA (Digital Living Network Alliance) technology to stream media files (videos, photos, music) wirelessly from

DLNA-compatible devices such as NAS drives, media servers, and smartphones/tablets to the projector. Access the projector's media player or compatible apps to browse and playback streamed media content seamlessly.

By leveraging wireless connectivity options such as Wi-Fi, Bluetooth, screen mirroring, and DLNA, users can enjoy versatile multimedia capabilities, seamless content sharing, and enhanced connectivity with external devices on the AWOL LTV-3500 Pro projector. Explore, connect, and stream wirelessly for an immersive and connected entertainment experience from various sources and devices.

Chapter 6: Maintenance and Care

Proper cleaning and maintenance are essential to ensure optimal performance, longevity, and visual clarity of the AWOL LTV-3500 Pro projector. This section provides comprehensive cleaning and maintenance tips to keep the projector in top condition and maximize its lifespan.

1. Cleaning the Exterior

Regularly clean the exterior surfaces of the projector to remove dust, dirt, fingerprints, and smudges. Use a soft, dry microfiber cloth to gently wipe the projector's casing, lens, and control buttons. Avoid using abrasive materials, harsh chemicals, or excessive pressure when cleaning to prevent scratches or damage to the surface.

2. Cleaning the Lens

Maintaining a clean lens is crucial for sharp and clear image projection. Follow these steps to clean the projector lens effectively:

- Power off the projector and allow it to cool down before cleaning.

- Use a lens brush or air blower to remove loose dust particles from the lens surface.
- Gently wipe the lens with a lens cleaning cloth or lens cleaning solution specifically designed for optical lenses.
- Start from the center of the lens and move outward in a circular motion to remove smudges or residue.
- Avoid touching the lens with bare fingers to prevent oil and dirt transfer.
- Repeat the cleaning process if necessary until the lens is clean and free of debris.

3. Air Vent Maintenance

Ensure proper airflow and ventilation by keeping the projector's air vents and filters clean. Dust and debris accumulation can restrict airflow, leading to overheating and performance issues. Follow these steps to maintain air vents:

- Power off the projector and unplug it from the power source.

- Locate the air intake and exhaust vents on the projector's casing.
- Use a soft brush or compressed air canister to remove dust and dirt buildup from the vents.
- Check and clean the air filter (if applicable) according to the manufacturer's instructions. Replace or clean the filter regularly to maintain optimal airflow and cooling efficiency.

4. Storage and Transport

When not in use, store the projector in a clean, dust-free environment away from direct sunlight, extreme temperatures, and humidity. Use a protective carrying case or cover to safeguard the projector during storage or transport. Avoid exposing the projector to moisture, liquids, or physical impact that may cause damage.

5. Lamp Replacement

Monitor the projector's lamp usage hours and replace the lamp when necessary to maintain optimal brightness and image quality. Follow the manufacturer's guidelines and instructions for lamp replacement, including proper handling and disposal of old lamps. Allow the projector to cool down completely before replacing the lamp to avoid burns or injuries.

6. Software Updates

Regularly check for firmware updates and software upgrades for the projector to ensure compatibility, performance improvements, and bug fixes. Follow the manufacturer's instructions for downloading and installing updates via USB or network connection.

7. Professional Maintenance

For complex issues, technical problems, or servicing requirements, contact authorized service centers or technicians for professional maintenance and repairs. Avoid disassembling or tampering with internal components of the projector without proper expertise and training.

By following these cleaning and maintenance tips, users can prolong the lifespan, preserve image quality, and ensure reliable performance of the AWOL LTV-3500 Pro projector for long-term enjoyment and usage. Regular maintenance practices contribute to optimal projector functionality and user satisfaction.

Troubleshooting Common Issues

Troubleshooting common issues with the AWOL LTV-3500 Pro projector is essential for resolving technical problems, optimizing performance, and ensuring a seamless viewing experience. This section provides comprehensive troubleshooting steps for common projector issues encountered by users.

1. No Power or Power Indicator Light

If the projector does not power on or the power indicator light does not illuminate, follow these troubleshooting steps:

- Check the power cable connection to ensure it is securely plugged into a working power outlet.
- Verify that the power outlet is functioning by testing with another device.
- Press the power button on the projector or the remote control to turn it on.
- If the projector still does not power on, check for any visible damage to the power cord or power supply unit. Replace damaged components as needed.
- Reset the projector by unplugging it from the power source, waiting for a few minutes, and then plugging it back in.

2. No Image Displayed or Blank Screen

If the projector powers on but does not display any image or shows a blank screen, try the following troubleshooting steps:

- Check the video source connection (HDMI, VGA, etc.) between the projector and the input device (laptop, Blu-ray player, gaming console, etc.). Ensure the cables are securely connected.
- Select the correct input source on the projector using the remote control or on-screen menu. Switch between different input sources to test for signal detection.
- Adjust the projector's focus and zoom settings to ensure a clear image projection.
- Verify that the input device is powered on and transmitting a video signal. Test the input device with another display to confirm functionality.
- If using a laptop or computer, check the display settings (resolution, refresh rate) and adjust them if necessary to match the projector's specifications.
- Replace the video cables or try using different input ports on the projector to rule out cable or port issues.

3. Poor Image Quality or Distorted Image

If the projected image appears blurry, distorted, or has poor quality, follow these troubleshooting steps:

- Clean the projector lens and remove any dust or smudges that may be affecting image clarity.
- Adjust the focus, zoom, and keystone correction settings on the projector to fine-tune the image.
- Check the projector's lamp usage hours and replace the lamp if it is nearing the end of its lifespan. A worn-out lamp can affect brightness and image quality.
- Ensure the input device's display settings (resolution, aspect ratio) are compatible with the projector's native resolution and aspect ratio.
- Test different video sources and content to determine if the issue persists across all inputs or specific sources.

- Check for any firmware updates or software upgrades for the projector and install them if available.

4. Audio Issues (No Sound or Low Volume)

If experiencing audio problems such as no sound or low volume levels, try the following troubleshooting steps:

- Check the audio cable connection between the projector and external speakers or audio devices. Ensure the cables are securely plugged in.
- Adjust the volume settings on both the projector and external audio devices to increase the volume output.
- Verify that the audio source (video file, streaming content) has sound and is not muted.
- Test the audio output with different audio sources and content to determine if the issue is with specific files or sources.

- If using Bluetooth speakers or headphones, ensure they are paired and connected properly to the projector.
- Check the projector's audio settings and adjust equalizer settings, audio modes, and speaker output configurations as needed for optimal sound quality.

5. Remote Control Malfunction

If the projector's remote control is not functioning correctly or is unresponsive, try the following troubleshooting steps:

- Replace the remote control batteries with fresh ones and ensure they are inserted correctly.
- Check for any obstructions or blockages between the remote control and the projector's infrared (IR) receiver. Clear any obstacles that may interfere with the signal.

- Test the remote control within close proximity to the projector to ensure the IR signal is reaching the receiver.
- If available, use the on-screen menu or buttons on the projector to access settings and functions as an alternative to the remote control.
- Consider using a universal remote control compatible with the projector if the original remote control continues to malfunction.

6. Overheating or Fan Noise

If the projector overheats or emits excessive fan noise during operation, follow these troubleshooting steps:

- Ensure the projector is placed in a well-ventilated area with sufficient airflow around the air intake and exhaust vents.
- Check for any dust or debris accumulation inside the projector's vents and air filters.

Use a soft brush or compressed air canister to clean the vents and filters.

- Avoid blocking the projector's ventilation pathways or placing it near heat sources that can contribute to overheating.
- Monitor the projector's operating temperature and usage hours to prevent prolonged use in high-temperature environments.
- If the projector continues to overheat or exhibit fan noise, contact authorized service centers or technicians for professional maintenance and inspection.

By following these troubleshooting steps and guidelines, users can effectively identify and resolve common issues encountered with the AWOL LTV-3500 Pro projector, ensuring optimal performance, functionality, and user satisfaction. Regular maintenance, proper setup, and troubleshooting practices contribute to a seamless and enjoyable viewing experience with the projector.

Chapter 7: Advanced Settings and Customization

Accessing and adjusting advanced settings on the AWOL LTV-3500 Pro projector allows users to fine-tune various parameters, customize preferences, and optimize performance based on specific viewing preferences and requirements. This section provides detailed guidance on how to access and adjust advanced settings on the projector for enhanced functionality and personalized user experience.

1. Accessing Advanced Settings Menu

To access the advanced settings menu on the LTV-3500 Pro projector, follow these steps:

- Power on the projector and ensure it is connected to a video source (e.g., laptop, Blu-ray player, gaming console).
- Use the remote control to navigate the on-screen menu.

- Press the "Menu" or "Settings" button on the remote control to open the main settings menu.
- Navigate to the "Advanced Settings" or "Setup" section within the menu options. The exact location of advanced settings may vary depending on the projector model and firmware version.

2. Picture Settings

Within the advanced settings menu, users can access a range of picture settings to adjust image quality, color accuracy, brightness, contrast, sharpness, and color temperature. Explore the following picture settings options:

- Brightness: Adjusts the overall brightness level of the projected image.
- Contrast: Controls the difference between light and dark areas for improved contrast.
- Color Temperature: Selects the color temperature mode (e.g., Cool, Warm, Standard) for accurate color reproduction.

- Sharpness: Enhances image sharpness and clarity by adjusting edge details.
- Color Settings: Fine-tunes color saturation, hue, and tint for vibrant and accurate color rendering.
- Aspect Ratio: Selects the aspect ratio (e.g., 16:9, 4:3) to match the content source for optimal viewing.

3. Audio Settings

In the advanced settings menu, users can access audio settings to adjust volume levels, equalizer settings, audio modes, and speaker configurations. Explore the following audio settings options:

- Volume: Adjusts the overall volume level of the projector's built-in speakers or connected audio devices.
- Equalizer: Customizes sound frequencies (e.g., bass, treble) for balanced audio output.

- Audio Modes: Selects preset audio modes (e.g., Standard, Music, Movie, Game) for different content types.
- Speaker Configuration: Configures speaker output settings (e.g., stereo, surround sound) for optimal audio performance.

4. System Settings

The advanced settings menu also includes system settings options to customize projector behavior, input/output configurations, language settings, network settings, firmware updates, and system information. Explore the following system settings options:

- Input Source: Selects the input source (e.g., HDMI, VGA, USB) for video and audio input from external devices.
- Network Settings: Configures Wi-Fi, Ethernet, and network connectivity settings for online access, firmware updates, and streaming services.

- Language Settings: Chooses the display language for on-screen menus and messages.
- Firmware Updates: Checks for and installs firmware updates to ensure compatibility, performance enhancements, and bug fixes.
- System Information: Displays projector information, firmware version, lamp usage hours, and network status.

5. Keystone Correction and Projection Mode

Advanced settings may include keystone correction options to correct image distortion caused by angled projection surfaces. Users can adjust vertical and horizontal keystone settings for a square and aligned image projection. Additionally, explore projection mode options such as front projection, rear projection, and ceiling mount configurations for flexible installation setups.

6. Save and Apply Settings

After adjusting advanced settings according to preferences, users can save and apply the settings to the projector. Navigate to the "Save" or "Apply" option within the advanced settings menu to store customized settings profiles for future use. This allows users to quickly access preferred settings configurations without the need for manual adjustments each time.

7. Resetting Settings

If desired, users can reset the projector's settings to default factory settings or specific preset configurations. This is useful for troubleshooting, starting fresh, or reverting to standard settings. Navigate to the "Reset" or "Factory Reset" option within the advanced settings menu to perform a settings reset.

By accessing and adjusting advanced settings on the AWOL LTV-3500 Pro projector, users can personalize image and audio settings, configure system preferences, and optimize projector performance for an immersive and tailored viewing experience. Explore and experiment with advanced settings to fine-tune projector settings according to specific viewing preferences and requirements.

Customizing User Preferences

Customizing user preferences on the AWOL LTV-3500 Pro projector allows for a personalized viewing experience tailored to individual preferences and requirements. This section delves into the various aspects of customizing user preferences on the projector, including picture and audio settings, input configurations, network settings, language preferences, and user profiles.

1. Picture Settings Customization

One of the key aspects of customizing user preferences on the projector is adjusting picture settings for optimal image quality and viewing comfort. Users can fine-tune various picture settings such as brightness, contrast, color temperature, sharpness, and color settings to achieve the desired visual experience. Customizing picture settings allows users to enhance image clarity, color accuracy, and overall viewing pleasure based on personal preferences.

2. Audio Settings Customization

In addition to picture settings, users can customize audio settings to optimize sound quality and audio output according to their preferences. Adjusting volume levels, equalizer settings, audio modes, and speaker configurations allows users to create a personalized audio experience for movies, music, gaming, and other content types. Customizing audio settings enhances the immersive nature of the viewing experience and ensures clear and balanced sound output.

3. Input Configurations

Customizing input configurations on the projector enables users to seamlessly connect and switch between different input sources such as HDMI, VGA, USB, and audio inputs. Users can prioritize input sources, rename input labels for easy identification, and adjust input settings for compatibility with external devices. Customizing input configurations streamlines the connectivity process and facilitates hassle-free access to multimedia content.

4. Network Settings Customization

For users who utilize network connectivity features, customizing network settings is essential for seamless online access, firmware updates, streaming services, and networked content sharing. Configuring Wi-Fi, Ethernet, DNS settings, and network security preferences allows users to establish a stable and secure network connection tailored to their network environment. Customizing network settings ensures reliable connectivity and enhances the projector's online capabilities.

5. Language Preferences

The projector's language preferences feature enables users to select their preferred display language for on-screen menus, messages, and settings. Customizing language preferences ensures that users can navigate and interact with the projector's interface in their preferred language, enhancing usability and accessibility for international users or multilingual environments.

6. User Profiles and Profiles Management

Some projectors offer user profile functionalities that allow multiple users to create personalized profiles with customized settings and preferences. Users can save and manage their settings profiles, including picture settings, audio settings, input configurations, network settings, and language preferences. User profiles management simplifies the process of switching between different user preferences and ensures a tailored viewing experience for each user.

7. Save and Apply Customized Preferences

After customizing user preferences, users can save and apply their customized settings to the projector. Saving customized preferences allows users to quickly access their preferred settings configurations without the need for manual adjustments each time. Applying customized preferences ensures a consistent and personalized viewing experience tailored to individual preferences.

By customizing user preferences on the AWOL LTV-3500 Pro projector, users can create a personalized and immersive viewing experience optimized for their specific preferences, content types, and viewing environments. Experimenting with different settings, profiles, and configurations allows users to fine-tune the projector's performance and enhance overall satisfaction with the viewing experience.

Firmware Updates and Upgrades

Firmware updates and upgrades play a crucial role in maintaining optimal performance, enhancing features, and ensuring compatibility with the latest technologies for projectors like the AWOL LTV-3500 Pro. This section explores the importance of firmware updates, the process of updating firmware, and the benefits of firmware upgrades for users.

Importance of Firmware Updates

Firmware serves as the operating system for projectors, controlling essential functions, settings, and performance parameters. Firmware updates are released periodically by manufacturers to address bugs, improve stability, enhance functionality, and introduce new features. Updating firmware is essential for ensuring smooth operation, resolving issues, and keeping the projector up-to-date with the latest advancements in technology.

Process of Updating Firmware

The process of updating firmware on the AWOL LTV-3500 Pro projector typically involves the following steps:

- Check for Updates: Begin by checking for available firmware updates for the projector. Manufacturers often provide updates through their official websites, support portals, or dedicated software applications.
- Download Firmware: Download the latest firmware version compatible with the projector model from the manufacturer's official source. Ensure to select the correct firmware version for the specific projector model and region.
- Prepare USB Drive: Transfer the downloaded firmware file to a USB flash drive formatted in FAT32 or exFAT file

system. Ensure that the USB drive has sufficient free space and is free from other files or data.

- Connect USB Drive: Insert the USB flash drive containing the firmware file into the USB port on the projector. Ensure that the projector is powered on and idle during the firmware update process.
- Initiate Update: Access the projector's settings menu using the remote control or on-screen interface. Navigate to the firmware update section within the settings menu and follow the on-screen instructions to initiate the firmware update process.
- Update Progress: The projector will automatically detect the firmware file on the USB drive and begin the update process. Monitor the update progress on the projector's display screen or LED indicators. Avoid interrupting the update process or powering off the projector during firmware installation.

- Completion and Reboot: Once the firmware update is complete, the projector may automatically reboot or prompt for a manual reboot. Follow any on-screen instructions to complete the update and restart the projector.

Benefits of Firmware Upgrades

Firmware upgrades offer several benefits to users of the AWOL LTV-3500 Pro projector:

- Bug Fixes: Firmware updates address software bugs, glitches, and performance issues identified in previous firmware versions, ensuring smoother operation and improved reliability.
- Stability and Compatibility: Upgrading firmware enhances system stability, compatibility with external devices, and interoperability with software applications, ensuring seamless functionality across different platforms and content sources.

- New Features: Firmware upgrades may introduce new features, functionalities, and enhancements to the projector, such as improved picture quality, audio performance, connectivity options, and user interface improvements.
- Security Patches: Firmware updates may include security patches, vulnerability fixes, and safeguards against cyber threats, protecting the projector and user data from potential security risks.
- Performance Optimization: Updated firmware may optimize system performance, energy efficiency, and resource utilization, leading to better overall performance and longevity of the projector.

Best Practices for Firmware Updates

To ensure successful firmware updates and upgrades on the AWOL LTV-3500 Pro projector, users should follow these best practices:

- Use Official Sources: Obtain firmware updates only from the manufacturer's official website, authorized support channels, or software update utilities provided by the manufacturer.
- Read Release Notes: Before updating firmware, review the release notes or documentation accompanying the firmware update to understand the changes, improvements, and instructions for installation.
- Backup Settings: Backup customized settings, user preferences, and profiles before initiating a firmware update to avoid data loss or configuration changes.
- Stable Power Supply: Ensure a stable power supply during the firmware update process to prevent interruptions, power failures, or data corruption.
- Allow Time for Update: Allocate sufficient time for the firmware update to complete without interruptions. Avoid using the projector for other tasks during the update process.

By regularly updating firmware and taking advantage of firmware upgrades, users can optimize the performance, functionality, and longevity of the AWOL LTV-3500 Pro projector, ensuring a reliable, feature-rich, and up-to-date viewing experience. Stay informed about firmware updates, follow best practices for installation, and enjoy the benefits of enhanced projector capabilities and improved user satisfaction.

Chapter 8: Tips and Tricks for Enhanced Viewing Experience

Optimizing screen size and placement is essential for maximizing the viewing experience and ensuring optimal image quality and clarity on the AWOL LTV-3500 Pro projector. This section provides valuable tips and guidelines for users to achieve the best possible screen size and placement for their viewing environment.

1. Consider Viewing Distance

The first tip for optimizing screen size and placement is to consider the viewing distance from the projector screen. The ideal viewing distance depends on the screen size and resolution of the projector. As a general guideline, for a 1080p resolution projector like the AWOL LTV-3500 Pro, a viewing distance of approximately 1.5 to 2 times the diagonal screen size is recommended for immersive viewing without pixelation or distortion.

2. Calculate Screen Size

Determine the optimal screen size based on the viewing distance and aspect ratio preferences. Use online calculators or formulas to calculate the diagonal screen size based on the viewing distance and aspect ratio (e.g., 16:9, 4:3). Ensure that the screen size is proportional to the viewing area and provides a comfortable viewing experience without straining the eyes or neck.

3. Adjust Projector Position

Position the projector at the correct distance and angle to achieve the desired screen size and aspect ratio. Use the projector's zoom and lens shift controls, if available, to fine-tune the image size and placement without compromising image quality. Avoid placing the projector too close or too far from the screen, as this can affect image clarity and focus.

4. Use Projection Screen or Wall

For optimal image quality and brightness, consider using a dedicated projection screen or a smooth, flat wall surface as the projection surface. Projection screens are designed to enhance image contrast, color accuracy, and viewing angles, resulting in a better overall viewing experience compared to projecting onto textured or uneven surfaces.

5. Minimize Ambient Light

To optimize screen visibility and image clarity, minimize ambient light in the viewing environment. Close curtains or blinds to block out external light sources, dim overhead lights, and create a darkened viewing space for enhanced contrast and color saturation. Ambient light can wash out the projected image and reduce overall viewing quality, especially in dark scenes or high-contrast content.

6. Use Screen Adjustment Tools

Utilize the projector's built-in screen adjustment tools and settings to optimize screen size, aspect ratio, keystone correction, and image alignment. Calibrate the projector's settings for sharpness, brightness, contrast, color temperature, and color balance to achieve the best possible image quality based on content type and viewing preferences.

7. Test Different Configurations

Experiment with different screen sizes, placements, and viewing angles to find the optimal configuration for your viewing environment. Test various projector positions, screen heights, and seating arrangements to determine the most comfortable and immersive viewing experience for different viewers and content types.

8. Consider Room Acoustics

In addition to screen size and placement, consider room acoustics and audio setup for a complete home theater experience. Position speakers strategically for balanced sound distribution, adjust audio settings for optimal sound quality, and incorporate acoustic treatments or sound-absorbing materials to minimize echoes and improve audio clarity.

By following these tips for optimizing screen size and placement, users can achieve the best possible viewing experience on the AWOL LTV-3500 Pro projector, with crisp, clear images, immersive visuals, and enhanced overall enjoyment of movies, games, and multimedia content. Experiment with different settings, configurations, and adjustments to fine-tune the projector setup for optimal performance and user satisfaction.

Enhancing 4K and HDR Content Playback

Enhancing 4K and HDR content playback on the AWOL LTV-3500 Pro projector involves optimizing settings, adjusting display configurations, and leveraging advanced features to deliver a premium viewing experience for high-resolution and high-dynamic-range (HDR) content. This section explores techniques and tips for enhancing 4K and HDR content playback on the projector.

1. Enable 4K Resolution

The first step in enhancing 4K content playback is to ensure that the projector is set to its native 4K resolution. Access the projector's display settings menu and select the appropriate resolution setting (e.g., 3840 x 2160 pixels for 4K UHD). Enabling 4K resolution ensures maximum detail, sharpness, and clarity for 4K content sources such as Blu-ray discs, streaming services, and gaming consoles.

2. HDR Compatibility and Settings

Verify that the projector supports HDR (High Dynamic Range) playback and configure HDR settings accordingly. HDR enhances color depth, contrast, and brightness range, resulting in more lifelike and vibrant images. Access the projector's HDR settings menu to enable HDR mode, adjust HDR brightness, and select HDR presets based on content type (e.g., HDR10, Dolby Vision).

3. Calibrate Color Settings

Calibrate color settings on the projector to achieve accurate color reproduction and HDR color gamut coverage. Adjust color temperature, color space settings (e.g., Rec. 709, DCI-P3), and color depth to match HDR content standards and deliver rich, nuanced colors with smooth gradients and natural skin tones.

4. Contrast and Black Levels

Fine-tune contrast and black levels on the projector to enhance HDR content playback.

Adjust gamma settings, dynamic contrast, and black level settings to optimize shadow detail, highlight brightness, and overall contrast performance. Balancing contrast and black levels ensures deep blacks, bright whites, and a wide dynamic range for HDR scenes.

5. HDR Tone Mapping

Utilize HDR tone mapping capabilities on the projector to optimize HDR content playback for different viewing environments and display capabilities. HDR tone mapping adjusts brightness, highlights, and shadows dynamically to preserve detail and prevent clipping, ensuring a balanced and immersive HDR viewing experience.

6. Upscaling and Enhancement

For non-native 4K content, utilize the projector's upscaling and enhancement features to upscale lower-resolution content to 4K quality. Enable upscaling algorithms, sharpness enhancement, and noise reduction techniques to improve image clarity, reduce artifacts, and enhance overall visual fidelity for HD and SD content sources.

7. Motion Handling and Frame Rate

Optimize motion handling and frame rate settings on the projector for smooth and fluid playback of 4K HDR content, especially fast-paced action scenes and gaming content. Adjust motion interpolation, frame smoothing, and refresh rate settings to reduce motion blur, judder, and lag for a more responsive and cinematic viewing experience.

8. HDR Brightness and Dynamic Range

Adjust HDR brightness and dynamic range settings to match the ambient light conditions and viewing preferences. Increase HDR brightness for well-lit environments and decrease it for dark room settings to maintain optimal HDR performance and visual impact without overexposure or loss of detail.

9. Viewing Environment Optimization

Create an optimal viewing environment by controlling ambient light, minimizing reflections, and optimizing seating arrangements for an immersive HDR viewing experience. Dim ambient light sources, use light-blocking curtains or shades, and position seating at the ideal viewing distance for maximum HDR impact and image quality.

10. Update Firmware and Software

Ensure that the projector's firmware and software are up to date to benefit from performance improvements, compatibility enhancements, and new features that enhance 4K and HDR content playback. Regularly check for firmware updates from the manufacturer and apply updates as needed to optimize projector performance.

By implementing these techniques and tips for enhancing 4K and HDR content playback on the AWOL LTV-3500 Pro projector, users can enjoy a cinematic, lifelike viewing experience with stunning visuals, vibrant colors, and immersive HDR effects. Experiment with different settings, adjust configurations based on content type, and fine-tune display parameters to achieve the best possible image quality and HDR performance on the projector.

Chapter 9: Frequently Asked Questions (FAQs)

Here are common questions and answers about the AWOL LTV-3500 Pro projector to provide users with comprehensive information and troubleshooting guidance:

1. What is the native resolution of the AWOL LTV-3500 Pro projector?

Answer: The AWOL LTV-3500 Pro projector features a native resolution of 3840 x 2160 pixels, also known as 4K Ultra HD resolution. This high-resolution display ensures sharp, detailed images for an immersive viewing experience.

2. Does the LTV-3500 Pro support HDR content playback?

Answer: Yes, the LTV-3500 Pro projector supports HDR (High Dynamic Range) content playback, including HDR10 and Dolby Vision formats. HDR enhances color depth, contrast, and brightness range for lifelike and vibrant visuals.

3. What is the brightness rating of the LTV-3500 Pro projector?

Answer: The LTV-3500 Pro projector is rated at 3,500 ANSI lumens, making it incredibly bright and suitable for use in various lighting conditions. The high brightness ensures clear and vivid images even in well-lit environments.

4. Can I connect external devices to the LTV-3500 Pro projector?

Answer: Yes, the LTV-3500 Pro projector offers multiple connectivity options, including HDMI ports, Ethernet connection, USB-A port, and optical audio input. Users can connect Blu-ray players, gaming consoles, streaming devices, and more for versatile content playback.

5. How do I update the firmware on the LTV-3500 Pro projector?

To update the firmware on the LTV-3500 Pro projector, follow these steps:

- Check for firmware updates on the manufacturer's official website or support portal.
- Download the latest firmware version compatible with your projector model.

- Transfer the firmware file to a USB flash drive formatted in FAT32 or exFAT.
- Insert the USB drive into the projector's USB port and navigate to the firmware update section in the settings menu.
- Follow the on-screen instructions to initiate and complete the firmware update process.

6. What are the key features of the LTV-3500 Pro projector?

Answer: The LTV-3500 Pro projector offers key features such as 4K resolution, HDR support, short-throw projection, high brightness, multiple connectivity options, advanced color settings, and compatibility with streaming devices.

7. How do I optimize screen size and placement for the LTV-3500 Pro projector?

Answer: To optimize screen size and placement, consider factors such as viewing distance, screen height, aspect ratio, ambient light conditions, and projector position. Use screen adjustment tools, calibration settings, and test different configurations for the best viewing experience.

8. What is the recommended maintenance for the LTV-3500 Pro projector?

Answer: Recommended maintenance for the LTV-3500 Pro projector includes regular cleaning of the lens, air vents, and external surfaces using a soft cloth. Avoid exposing the projector to extreme temperatures, humidity, or dust accumulation to ensure longevity and optimal performance.

9. Does the LTV-3500 Pro projector have built-in speakers?

Answer: Yes, the LTV-3500 Pro projector is equipped with built-in speakers to provide audio output. However, users can also connect external speakers or sound systems for enhanced audio quality and surround sound experience.

10. What is the warranty coverage for the LTV-3500 Pro projector?

Answer: The warranty coverage for the LTV-3500 Pro projector may vary depending on the manufacturer's terms and conditions. Users are advised to refer to the warranty documentation or contact customer support for specific warranty details and coverage.

These common questions and answers about the AWOL LTV-3500 Pro projector cover various aspects, features, connectivity options, maintenance tips, and troubleshooting guidelines to help users make informed decisions and optimize their viewing experience with the projector.

Conclusion

The AWOL LTV-3500 Pro projector stands out with its array of key features and benefits that elevate the viewing experience to new heights. Here's a recap of the key features and benefits that users can expect from this advanced projector:

1. 4K Ultra HD Resolution: Enjoy stunningly detailed and sharp images with the native 4K resolution of 3840 x 2160 pixels, providing an immersive visual experience for movies, games, and multimedia content.

2. HDR Support: Dive into vibrant and lifelike colors with HDR support, including HDR10 and Dolby Vision formats, enhancing contrast, brightness, and color depth for realistic visuals.

3. Short-Throw Projection: Set up the projector easily with short-throw projection capabilities, allowing for a large screen size even in limited

spaces without the need for complicated mounting systems.

4. High Brightness: Experience clear and vivid images even in well-lit environments with the projector's high brightness rating of 3,500 ANSI lumens, ensuring excellent visibility and image quality.

5. Versatile Connectivity: Connect external devices such as Blu-ray players, gaming consoles, streaming devices, and more via HDMI ports, Ethernet connection, USB-A port, and optical audio input for versatile content playback options.

6. Advanced Color Settings: Fine-tune color settings, color temperature, and color space options to achieve accurate color reproduction and HDR color gamut coverage, delivering rich and nuanced colors.

7. Built-in Speakers: Enjoy audio output directly from the projector with built-in speakers, or

connect external speakers or sound systems for enhanced audio quality and immersive sound experience.

The AWOL LTV-3500 Pro projector offers a compelling package of features, performance, and versatility that caters to the needs of discerning users looking for a premium home entertainment experience. With its 4K resolution, HDR support, short-throw capabilities, high brightness, and advanced color settings, this projector delivers exceptional visual quality and immersive viewing across various content types.

For users seeking a cinematic experience at home, the LTV-3500 Pro projector ticks all the boxes with its impressive specifications and user-friendly design. Whether you're watching movies, playing games, or streaming content, this projector provides a captivating and enjoyable viewing experience.

How to Stay Updated with Future Developments and Updates

To stay updated with future developments, firmware updates, and new features for the AWOL LTV-3500 Pro projector, follow these recommendations:

1. Manufacturer's Website: Regularly check the manufacturer's official website for product updates, firmware releases, and announcements regarding new features or improvements for the projector.

2. Customer Support: Contact customer support or technical assistance for the projector to inquire about firmware updates, troubleshooting tips, and any upcoming developments or enhancements.

3. User Communities: Join online forums, user communities, and social media groups dedicated to projectors and home entertainment systems. Engage with fellow users, share experiences, and

stay informed about the latest news and updates related to the LTV-3500 Pro projector.

4. Product Documentation: Refer to the product documentation, user manuals, and guides provided with the projector for detailed information about firmware updates, settings adjustments, and maintenance recommendations.

By staying proactive and keeping abreast of new developments and updates, users can ensure that their AWOL LTV-3500 Pro projector remains optimized, up-to-date, and delivers the best possible viewing experience over time.